The Stc
Snake

Written by Ian MacDonald

Illustrated by Lucy Semple and Ryan Ball

RISING ★ STARS

Sam was not well.

"You need to stay away from people for six weeks," said Doctor Larue.

It was no use trying to argue.

It was June. Sam's friends were out playing
in the park.
Sam thought they might forget him.
This will be rotten! thought Sam.

Sam's teacher had sent an art activity home.
Mum put out paint, glue, card and tissue paper,
but Sam just sat there.

"You could play your computer game?"
said Mum.

"All my games are stupid!" said Sam, throwing
himself onto the cushions.

"We could go to the woods later," said Mum.
"There won't be many people there."
That was true. Sam could still stick to Doctor
Larue's rules in the woods.

So after supper, Sam pulled on his trainers.
Once they were through the factory units, Sam
and his mum were soon out in the woods.

Sam ran along the path.

He pulled himself up on a big tree stump.

He dropped sticks into the river.

Then Sam stopped as still as a statue.
He had spotted something … something blue
that blinked at him from under a bush.
He bent over.

It was a stone.

On the stone someone had painted a white unicorn on a blue sky.

Under the stone was a note.

"It's a clue!" cried Sam.

"We must find the stone snake," said Mum.

Sam and Mum went back and forth until …

Taking a new path, they came to a little glade where wind chimes hung in the trees.

When the wind blows, the chimes play a tune!

And, curling in and out of the trees, were painted stones of every shape and size and hue. "It's the stone snake!" gasped Sam.

Sam put the unicorn stone at the end of
the snake.

Nearby, under a stack of flat stones, was a note.

Sam took a stone home to paint.
The next day, he added it to the snake.
As he painted the stones, the snake
got longer.

Then, one day, someone was there.
"Hello, I'm Prue," she said.

I like the stones.

"Please keep back," said Sam. "I have to stay away from people at the moment."

"That's too bad," she replied. "But we could use the snake to be friends."

Day after day, Sam and Prue added to the snake.
The friends kept apart, putting the stones they
had painted at each end.
They waved as they left each night.

The weeks passed, and the snake became longer and longer. Sam got better and better.
But on the day Sam could meet people again, the snake was missing!

Sadly, Sam turned for home. But then he saw something on the path.

The stone trail led home. Sam pushed open the gate. The garden was full of children. They had formed a human snake!

It's a friendship snake.

It's the best snake of all!

Phonics Practice

Say the sound and read the words.

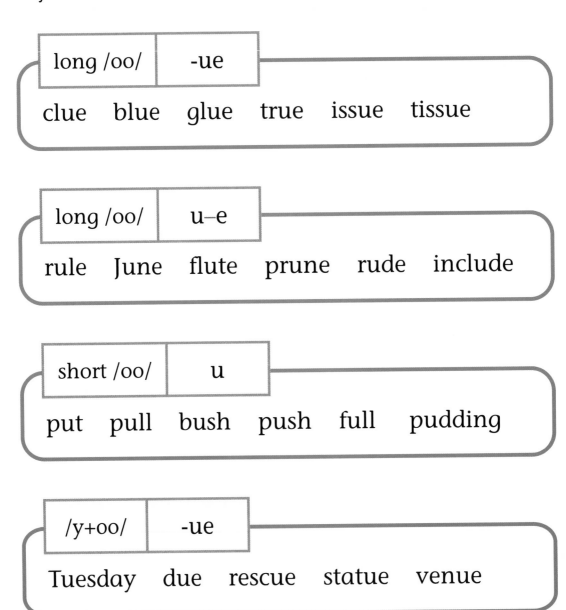

long /oo/	-ue

clue   blue   glue   true   issue   tissue

long /oo/	u–e

rule   June   flute   prune   rude   include

short /oo/	u

put   pull   bush   push   full   pudding

/y+oo/	-ue

Tuesday   due   rescue   statue   venue

Can you say your own sentences using some of the words on these pages?

What other words do you know that are spelled in these ways?

/y+oo/	u–e

cube   tube   use   cute   amused

/y+oo/	u

unit   music   tuba   human   duty

Common exception words

oh   their   people   Mr   Mrs   looked

We may say some words differently because of our accent.

Talk about the story

Answer the questions:

1 How many weeks did Sam have to stay away
   from people?

2 What was painted on the first stone Sam found?

3 What helped Sam and his mum find
   the stone snake?

4 How did the snake help Sam feel better?

5 Would you like to make a stone snake? Why?

6 How do you keep busy when you can't see
   your friends?

Can you retell the story in your own words?